YOU CAN

DO IT IN

SIX DAYS

Learn and Apply

The Creator's Principles

Edition 05

FOLLOWGOD ABOVE

DEDICATION

This book is dedicated to
FRIENDS AND PARTNERS
of APOSTLE FOLLOWGOD ABOVE

TABLE OF CONTENTS

FOLLOW GOD

My father was in the military when I was born. He was not a professing Christian then but he loved the things of God. He gave me the name BOHEJE meaning FOLLOWGOD. As I was growing up, I denounced the name because it was an obstruction to all the works the devil wanted to do through me.

Years later, I became born again and I took up the name and made it more pronounced by using the English version of it. Why? I was seeking the face of God and He revealed to me why He put the name in the heart of my father. God showed me how He wants me to follow Him and encourage others to do the same. This is the very pivot on which my whole life spins.

God wants you to be a great achiever. He wants you to do a thing within a set time that will shock your generation. He made the entire heaven and earth within six days to set a simple but proven standard for you to follow. The virtues and principles He employed at creation are for you to copy in order to achieve something monumental. The truth is, if you imitate His character and follow His ways, you will have His kind of accomplishments.

You take the likeness of the person you follow. "He that walketh with wise men shall be wise..." (Prov. 13:20). The person you follow can transform you to his kind of person. "And he (Jesus Christ) saith unto them, Follow me, and I will make you fishers of men" (Matt. 4:19). The truest way to follow God is to adopt His attitudes and to work according to His patterns.

YOU CAN DO IT IN SIX DAYS is a simple book; it is about believing God to have His kind of achievements by living the way He lived and working the way He worked when He made the Heaven and the earth. It is a book that will not leave you the same but transform you to a great achiever.

CHAPTER ONE

PREPARATION

Agood attitude gives you excellent mark anywhere in the world. The lack of it is your downfall whether you work in the most civilized city or in the remotest village.

Consider this table.

A for 1	B for 2	C for 3	D for 4	E for 5	F for 6	G for 7	H for 8	I for 9
J for 10	K for 11	L for 12	M for 13	N for 14	O for 15	P for 16	Q for 17	R for 18
S for 19	T for 20	U for 21	V for 22	W for 23	X for 24	Y for 25	Z for 26	

This is the word ATTITUDE. In the table, every alphabet in the word attitude has a number or numbers attached to it. Let's add the numbers that make the word attitude to see how much it will amount to. $^{A}1+ {}^{T}20+ {}^{T}20+ {}^{I}9+ {}^{T}20+ {}^{U}21+ {}^{D}4+ {}^{E}5= {}^{ATTITUDE}100$. Anywhere in the world, you are a hundred percent man, an excellent man, if you have a good attitude to life. This is the dominant reason why most achievers accomplish so much. Nothing stands you in good stead to accomplishing great things as the right attitude to work.

Our Lord Jesus Christ had the good attitude to work. He was in the earth He made and said, "I must work" (John 9:4). Every work attitude the Bible recorded about the Lord Jesus Christ when He was physically here on earth was the same at creation. He did not work differently at creation and at redemption. Hebrews 13:8 says, "Jesus Christ the same yesterday, and today, and forever".

One of the work attitudes we must adopt from the Almighty is enjoying preparation for achievement. Two things are very important here: to prepare, and to enjoy preparing. There is no great achiever that lacks these. God prepares and enjoys preparing adequately for His works. He promised redemption after the fall of man and He took approximately four thousand one hundred years to prepare.

The Lord Jesus Christ promised to prepare a place for the people who believe in Him and it has taken Him over two millennia and a decade.

> **Let not your heart be troubled: ye believe in God, believe also in me. In my Father's house are many mansions: if it were not so, I would have told you. I go to prepare a place for you. And if I go and prepare a place for you, I will come again, and receive you unto myself; that where I am, there ye may be also.**
> John 14:1-3

I so believe that rapture will take place immediately the Lord Jesus is through with His preparation of the PLACE. When the Lord Jesus Christ was here on earth to executive the redemption plan, He took thirty years to prepare and three and half years to work. Even though we cannot readily find figures to substantiate God's preparation for the formation of the Heaven and the earth,

His nature, as clearly revealed in the Scripture, proves it to be true. One or two millennia must have been spent on preparation for the construction of the universe.

The long period of time spent on preparation aptly shows that He also enjoys preparing for His spectacular works. You cannot do anything across years if you do not enjoy it. God takes millennia, centuries, decades and years to prepare for one thing and that proves His delight in preparation. You need to follow God in this way also; prepare and enjoy preparing to do something significant. You need to take quality time to prepare if what you want to achieve is not an anthill.

The truth is, if you take much time to prepare, you will take less time to perform. From all the examples of God's works, He takes much time to prepare and less time to do the actual work. He took six days to make what He must have taken one or two millennia to prepare for. It is like taking years to prepare a bomb that can destroy a city in few minutes. The Heaven and the earth and all that is in them came to existence from the womb of preparation.

Most achievers exhibit the same attitude to work; much time to prepare and least of time to perform. It was Abraham Lincoln who said, "Give me six hour to chop down a tree and I will spend the first four sharpening the axe." Wentworth Miller said, "Four months of preparation and about 12 hours of shooting turned into 30 seconds of screen time." You will spend much time and energy struggling to achieve a thing if you spend the least of time and effort to prepare.

The Bible says,

Since a dull ax requires great strength... If your ax is dull and you don't sharpen it, you have to work harder to use it. It is smarter to plan ahead.
Eccl. 10:10 NLT & TEV

The bane of most people is failing to sharpen their axes; failure to plan ahead and adequately work in advance. Achievement and failure are offspring of good preparation and the lack of it respectively. Robert H. Schuller said, "Spectacular achievement is preceded by unspectacular preparation." Don't you think it is really unspectacular to take millennia, centuries and decades to prepare for a project of six days? This is why God achieves the spectacular with the least of time.

If you do not take time to prepare for your goals in life, struggle becomes inevitable. It was Benjamin Franklin who said, "By failing to prepare, you are preparing to fail." Mike Murdock put it this way, "Failure to prepare is preparing to fail." It goes to mean that everyone on earth is preparing for something in life, either success or failure. God is always preparing for something mind-blowing; your choice is clear if you follow Him.

The ant is the wealthiest of insects and its top most key is long term preparation.

Go to the ant, O sluggard; consider her ways, and be wise. Without having any chief, officer or ruler, she prepares her food in summer, and gathers her sustenance in harvest. The ants are a people not strong, yet they prepare their meat in the summer.
Prov. 6:6-8 RSV, 30:25 KJV

There is no one that achieves great feats without first embarking on a thorough and conscientious preparation. If you have a goal in life, set a good time and prepare adequately for it. And if you know the joy of achieving your goals in life, do not prepare as though you are being punished. You need to prepare with excitement as though you have achieved it already. This is the attitude that does not give room for despair while you prepare for something magnificent.

Be a follower of God; make extraordinary preparation; leave no stone unturned; work out so many things in advance. God will surely send right opportunities to you and you will become the news in the ears of the world. Bobby Unser said, "Success is where preparation and opportunity meet." If you imitate God's kind of preparation, you will have His kind of achievement.

CHAPTER TWO

MOTIVATION

Over a decade ago, a young man was always coming to me to complain about his parents' unsupportiveness to his cause. But I kept encouraging him in the Lord. One day, I got weary of his complaints and I say a word that changed his life. I told him, "I wish you can see yourself as an orphan." He was very angry and left my office. He thought I wished his parents death.

After some weeks, he accepted to be an "orphan" and came back to me. I showed him how to start a business without money and prayed for him. He went to a wholesaler and persuasively negotiated business. He got goods, sold them and faithfully returned the wholesaler's money. He continued until his profit became enough capital for the same business. This was where his prosperity began.

Be a self-motivated orphan. Take your eyes off people and trust God to use you to encourage yourself. Do not wait for the cheers of others. Appoint yourself a motivator to yourself; anything you need anybody to do to encourage you in life, do it for yourself. If you know how to cheer yourself, you can achieve anything. Self-motivation is crucial to accomplishing great things in this life.

Who was there to encourage God when He made the Heaven and the earth? Nobody! So, what do you think He did when He met the earth as a "formless mass cloaked in darkness"? (Gen. 1:2 NLT). I believe He encouraged Himself in Himself. David, a man after God's heart did the same in his moment of distress. God encouraged Himself in Himself; David encouraged himself in his God.

> Look at it,
> **So David and his men came to the city, and, behold, it was burned with fire; and their wives, and their sons, and their daughters, were taken captives. Then David and the people that were with him lifted up their voice and wept, until they had no more power to weep.**
> **And David's two wives were taken captives, Ahinoam the Jezreelitess, and Abigail the wife of Nabal the Carmelite. And David was greatly distressed; for the people spake of stoning him, because the soul of all the people was grieved, every man for his sons and for his daughters: but David ENCOURAGED HIMSELF in the LORD his God.**
> 1 Sam. 30:3-6

Let the encouragement you give yourself be such sufficient that you will not need a little from any other person. Internal motivation should be everything to you. If you do not motivate yourself well enough, external motivation will never be sufficient to achieve anything noteworthy. A total dependence on the encouragement from outside is the very reason why many people achieve nothing worthwhile in life. You see, internal encouragement is the power of great achievement.

Shiv Khera told a story in his book, *You Can Win:* "There was a man who made his living selling balloons at a fair. He had balloons of different colours. Whenever business was slow, he would release a helium-filled balloon into the air. When the children saw the balloon go up, they all wanted one. They would come up to him, buy a balloon and his sales would go up. All day, he continued to release a balloon whenever the sales slowed down.

One day, the balloon man felt someone tugging at his jacket, he turned around and a little boy asked, 'If you release the black balloon, would that also fly?' Moved by the boy's seeking concern, the man replied gently, 'Son, it is not the colour of the balloon, it is what's inside that makes it go up.'" What takes the balloon up is the air inside. It is internal motivation that first of all takes you up.

If a balloon is airless, it must take a whirlwind for it to go up; and when the wind ceases, it must return to base. People devoid of a rich inward motivation cannot go up at all; you hardly find a whirlwind motivation anywhere nowadays. If you see anyone rising and making great advancement, it is almost hundred percent as a result of self-motivation. The choice is yours! You could choose to encourage yourself in your God or wait endlessly in vain for others to motivate you and push you to your next level.

> When no one believed Him, He said of Himself
> **The Spirit of the Lord is upon me, because he hath anointed me to preach the gospel to the poor; he hath sent me to heal the brokenhearted, to preach deliverance to the captives, and recovering of sight to the blind, to set at liberty them that are bruised, To preach the acceptable year of the Lord.**

See the response of his people? "And he closed the book, and he gave it again to the minister, and sat down. And the eyes of all them that were in the synagogue were FASTENED on him" (Luke 4:20). He went ahead and told them, "This day is this scripture fulfilled in your ears" (Luke 4:21). There are times that you will be the only one by yourself and you must support yourself.

> When Eliab harasses you,
> **Why camest thou down hither? and with whom hast thou left those few sheep in the wilderness? I know thy pride, and the naughtiness of thine heart; for thou art come down that thou mightest see the battle.**
> 1 Sam. 17:28

> And Saul takes you for granted,
> **Thou art not able to go against this Philistine to fight with him: for thou art but a youth, and he a man of war from his youth.**
> 1 Sam. 17:33

Be an inspiration to yourself, "And David said unto Saul, Thy servant kept his father's sheep, and there came a lion, and a bear, and took a lamb out of the flock: And I went out after him, and smote him, and delivered it out of his mouth: and when he arose against me, I caught him by his beard, and smote him, and slew him" (1 Sam. 17:34-35)

"Thy servant slew both the lion and the bear: and this uncircumcised Philistine shall be as one of them, seeing he hath defied the armies of the living God. David said moreover, The LORD that delivered me out of the paw of the lion, and out of the paw of the bear, he will deliver me out of the hand of this

Philistine" (1 Sam. 17:36-37). When everyone talks down your efforts, be the only one to confidently inspire yourself.

When everyone makes you feel you are a rat, do everything good to quicken and awaken the lion in you. When everyone says you cannot do it, say to yourself, "I can do all things through Christ which strengtheneth me" (Phil. 4:13). When they shout you down, don't shut up, "cried the more a great deal" (Mark 10:48). When everyone think you are finished, be the only one saying "I think myself happy" (Acts 26:2).

As far as you are pursuing your goals in life, succeed in motivating yourself. You will surely achieve great feats if you know how to inspire yourself. Elisha encouraged himself until he secured the "double portion" of Elijah's anointing. Everyone, including his master, did not inspire him but he succeeded in inspiring himself. No one encouraged him but everyone bowed to him when he returned as an achiever.

> The Bible says,
> **And when the sons of the prophets which were to view at Jericho saw him, they said, The spirit of Elijah doth rest on Elisha. And they came to meet him, and bowed themselves to the ground before him.**
> 2 Kings 2:15

If you give up because you have no one to encourage you, you will be the one that will lose out in the future. Imagine that Elisha gave in to the discouraging voice of the people; he would have existed as an inconsequential fellow. Imbibe the self-motivating attitude of the achievers. Be the resolute and constant motivator of yourself. This will certainly translate to so much strength to work and accomplish amazing feats.

CHAPTER THREE

OVERSIGHT

Let us take a look at a few verses of the Scripture that perfectly enunciate the concept of oversight as a base of our emphasis. "I am the LORD that maketh all things; that stretcheth forth the heavens ALONE; that spreadeth abroad the earth by MYSELF... I ALONE stretched out the heavens; when I made the earth, no one helped me... All things were made by me; I ALONE stretched out the heavens. By MYSELF I made the earth and everything in it" (Isaiah 44:24).

Isaiah 45:18 also says, "God HIMSELF that formed the earth and made it..." When it comes to oversight, ant is one creature that has imitated God so well. Little wonder, the Almighty directs humanity to go and learn her attitude to work. "Go to the ant, thou sluggard; consider her ways, and be wise: Which having no guide, overseer, or ruler, Provideth her meat in the summer, and gathereth her food in the harvest" (Prov. 6:6-11).

It was Frank Tyger who said, "Your future depends on many things, but mostly on you." Like the Almighty, the ant does not depend on anyone to achieve her goals; she takes charge of herself and her affairs. The Bible says she has no guide, overseer or ruler. So, she does for herself what a guide, an overseer and a ruler would have done for her. She takes full responsibility for her achievement. She does not live with the mind that someone else will foot her bills.

What should a guide do for the ant? It is to show her the way to her destination. The ant does this for herself; she does not wait for any guide to go anywhere. What should an overseer do for the ant? It is to encourage her as she pursues her goals. The ant does this for herself; she is a self-motivated achiever. It was Socrates who counselled, "Let him that would move the world first move himself." The ant moves herself; she does not wait to be pushed by someone else.

What should the ant need a ruler for? A ruler compels people to do things in order to meet his goals. The ant does not have a ruler but she has goals. She therefore made herself a ruler over herself. She compels herself to work in order to reach her seasonal targets. One of the strengths of the ant is her ability to run relentlessly for 24 hours. Like the Almighty God, she neither sleeps nor slumbers in the pursuit of her goals.

I believe God knows that the ant shares a common ground with Him in work ethics that is why He instructed man to learn from her. Imagine that God was waiting for help from others before He formed the Heaven and the earth, He would have been disappointed. He made all things by Himself alone. He said, "By myself I made the earth and everything in it. I alone stretched out the heavens; when I made the earth, no one helped me" (Isaiah 44:24).

You need to follow God in this way. Learn to be everything to yourself; not that you will reject help but be poised to achieve your goals without it. No one helped God yet He realized His dream. I believe God will send you helpers and helps but make nobody and nothing the determinants of your accomplishments. Make God the constant factor and you the only variable factor to your achievement in life. Let no man say you failed because he did not support you.

Something happened in the early days of my ministry and every time I remember it, a well of gratitude springs up in my heart. An old prophet told my associate ministers that they are the reason for the speedy rise of my ministry, and that if they desert me, everything will crumble. From that moment, the young men started misbehaving and finally left one after another. But their departure only ushered the ministry to a greater dimension of breakthrough. And since then, we keep moving from glory to glory.

I have never hung my progress on the shoulders of anyone. I believe in God and His ability at work in me. As a matter of principle, I deliberately chose not to make people the determinants of my success. I do appreciate the great contribution of people to my ministry but I have learnt to make my plans having God and myself in mind. This is the very reason why I cannot be disappointed with anyone as I work towards achieving my goals in life.

You need to also come to the point where you can say like the Almighty, "By myself I made...I alone made...no one helped me". If you leave your achievements on the shoulders of others, you will do nothing of significance in this life. Just make up your mind to do it by yourself; and if help comes from others, thank God. It is this unflinching commitment to her own affairs that gave ant a conspicuous place in the greatest book ever written. And if you can imbibe this virtue, the sky will suddenly become too close to be your limit.

The truth is, it is when you start achieving great things that others come to be a part of it. Simon Peter had a turnaround in his fishing business before partners came. The ant finds a big piece of meat before others join her to drag it home. If you wait for others for your initial achievements, you will wait for life. There are people who have done nothing about their callings from God because they are waiting endlessly for others who may never show.

You see, God does not give His assignment to a group. No. He calls a man to do His work and He calls him alone. The LORD said, "Look unto Abraham your father, and unto Sarah that bare you: for I called him ALONE, and blessed him, and increased him" (Isaiah 51:2). If you know God called you alone, start doing the work alone and others will be your blessing and increase.

CHAPTER FOUR

PRUDENCE

Achievers are generous but not reckless. The Maker of the Heaven and the earth was generous and prudent. He constructed the entire universe and He gave no room for waste. Everything available to Him was used completely and nothing was left to waste. In other words, all the resources at His disposal were judiciously utilized. There was no purposeless or useless piece of any element left anywhere in the universe because everything was put to good use.

Take a walk to any construction site and you will hold your breath in consternation to see how most people waste resources for sheer lack of prudence. The Maker of all things said to His disciples, "Gather up the fragments that remain, that nothing be lost" (John 6:12). Left for the disciples, "the fragments" meant nothing. To God, the fragments were twelve baskets of harvest for the sower. God worked with this same nothing-be-lost mentality when He made the universe.

If you want to have God's kind of achievement, you must imbibe this virtue of prudence. You need to always use all the resources God makes available to you efficiently. No waster of divine resources will enjoy a continuous supply from God; and whatever stops your supply invariably cripples your opportunity for greater achievements. You need to also build in the nothing-be-lost mentality to your work life. Be sure that nothing is wasted; nothing is left to go bad; and nothing stands useless.

Time is the most volatile of all resources of life. Like all the resources available to God, He made the most of His time. In other words, He was prudent in the use of His time. He did not lose a nano second while preparing and forming the Heaven and the earth. You need to follow God and ensure prudence in the usage of your time. What can you do under one week without losing time to sleep and vain activities?

You have wasted your entire existence if you do not know what you have done with your time on earth. The most painful thing about time is that it goes away whether you use it meaningfully or not. You get older by every minute that passes, and every day that goes by brings you closer to your expiring date. You can put a hold to other resources but not on time. Any fragment of time that is wasted is gone forever.

You cannot be better than what you use your time to do. Achievers spend their time on purpose; they know what they do with each hour. If you want to be an achiever of great feats, you must always know what your 24 hours go for. The most unfortunate thing we see in this part of the world is that people spend days, weeks, months, and even years doing nothing worthwhile. It is tragic when a man cannot say what he did with an entire year.

If your time does not count to you, you will not count in life. Time is one of your most valuable resources and you need to fully maximize every bit of it. You see, there is a disparity in the amount of money, level of ability, measure of grace that we have but we all share a certain commonality which is the gauge of time. Any great achiever on earth has the same 24 hours the poorest man on the street has. It is all about what each person does with his own time.

A wise person said, "Time is the general currency on the earth, shared equally to all men." The hours of the day are given to all equally but people are unequal for the choice of the usage of the common time. Pastor W. F. Kumuyi said, "The value of time is in what you achieve within it." Henry W. Longfellow said, "The height which great men reached and kept were not attained by sudden flight. It is while their companions slept that they kept toiling upwards into the sky."

> In his time, Moses prayed,
> **Teach us to make the most of our time, so that we may grow in wisdom**.
> **Teach us to number our days and recognize how few they are; help us to spend them as we should.**
> Psalms 90:12 NLT & TLB

Let it be your absolute resolve to make the most of your time. There is a judicious way of spending your time and that is spending it in God's way, making the most of every minute. Before you rest each night, ask yourself: What have I done with my time today? Just imagine how God felt after each day of the creation; I believe it was a great feeling of fulfillment. That is what happens when you set goals and achieve them within a given time frame. Be prudent with your time. Work long enough and take a time-bound rest.

Do not be a sleeping giant whose hundred percent achievements are in ordinary dreams. If you sleep, you will continue to dream;

but if you work hard, you will continue to achieve great things. It is so painful to discover that sleep takes the greater portion of the precious resource of time in the lives of most people globally. Most people just live to sleep, and not rest to live. The truth is, achievers do not sleep; they only take a rest. Whatever you do in bed above 20 percent of 24 hours, you sleep, not rest.

Twenty percent of 24 hours is 4 hours 48 minutes. Whatever you do in bed above this is called sleep, small death, killer of time and opportunities. Where time is concerned, most people die small in every 24 hours. This daily sleep-death affects people's lifespan, productivity and accomplishments in life. Actually, most people died long before they stopped breathing. They died in the extra hours they spend sleeping.

Psalms 90:10 put the average life span of a man at 70 years. Several phases of your existence share these years. Childhood takes up at least 13 years. To sleep for maximum of 6 hours in every 24 hours takes up another 17 years. You are left with 40 years for your training, work and leisure. Minus training and leisure, you are left with less than 15 years to do all that God ordained you for.

Now, consider a man that sleeps for 9 hours daily, he spends over 25 years of his lifetime on earth to sleep. Hence, he is left with a total of 8 years for the pursuit of destiny. To sleep more than 6 hours in every 24 hours is anti-success. It is to accept to spend more than 17 years out of the 70 years of existence only sleeping.

An African international businessman said, "I take a 4 hour rest daily". If other areas of his life are well taken care of, why wouldn't he achieve so much?

It is even more painful that while a man sleeps for 25 years out of his 70 years, he still does not commit the 8 years left to any worthy cause. Start to live like great achievers; rest after others have slept and still wake before them. The Bible says, "...her lights burn late into the night...she gets up before dawn..." (Prov. 31:15, 18). When Jesus was on earth, He worked late into the night and woke very early the next day to continue His work.

> Look at it,
> **And at even, when the sun did set, they brought unto him all that were diseased, and them that were possessed with devils. And all the city was gathered together at the door. And he healed many that were sick of divers diseases, and cast out many devils; and suffered not the devils to speak, because they knew him. And in the morning, rising up a great while before day, he went out, and departed into a solitary place, and there prayed.**
> Mark 1:32-35

This was the same work attitude during the formation of the Heaven and the earth. You cannot be a man given to sleep and achieve as much as God intended that you should achieve. It was Theodore Roosevelt that said, "Nine-tenths of wisdom is being wise in time."

If sleep does not have any negative impact on the dimension of what you could accomplish, the only wise God would not have warned, "Love not sleep, lest thou come to poverty..." (Prov. 20:13).

If you know what you do with your time while others sleep or engage in frivolous activities, you will be an achiever in the land. If you stay awake, be sure you are working on something that adds value to your life. Never deny yourself sleep and be engaged in things that have no bearing with your goals for life. Why will you stay awake at night only to watch one movie after another? If I have done so, this book will not be in your hand. If God had done so, you would not have been in existence.

CHAPTER FIVE

REFRESH

When I was a teenager, I followed my Dad to farm and worked all day. At that time he had retired from the Nigerian Army and he was a dyed-in-the-wool workaholic. My siblings hated going to farm with him because it was always work and work until sundown. I seemed to be the only child that enjoyed his workaholism back then, and little wonder he loved me. He wrote my names as next of kin in all his deeds.

The all-day work notwithstanding, he would stop to take his meal, usually roasted yam and palm oil. Then after thirty minutes to one hour, he would resume the second phase of an intensive work. When the Bible says, God "rested", I believe, it is in this context (Gen. 2:2). God did not stop working; He ceased from His work to refresh. When armies retreat, it is not because the war is over; it is for reinforcement for more tactical advance. In football, halftime is not the end of the game; it is to regain strength and restrategize for victory.

When the Bible says the Maker of the Heaven and the earth rested, it was not referring to sleep but a brief cease from work.

"The LORD, which made heaven and earth...neither slumber nor sleep" (Ps. 121:2-4). The truth is, sleep is the preserve of the flesh; spirits don't sleep. To God, rest means a brief stay off from work. "For he that is entered into his rest, he also hath ceased from his own works, as God did from his" (Heb. 4:10).

> Look at this,
> **Thus the heavens and the earth were finished, and all the host of them. And on the seventh day God ended his work which he had made; and he RESTED on the seventh day from all his work which he had made.**
> Gen. 2:1-2

You need to understand that God was not exhausted in strength or in wisdom. He did not rest to recoup strength or restrategize. The virtue that went out of Him for the formation of the Heaven and the earth was nothing compared to His reserve (Luke 8:46). He rested to teach us how to live as spirits, having souls and living in bodies.

> **Work six days only, for the seventh day is a special day to remind you of my covenant - a weekly reminder forever of my promises to the people of Israel. For in six days the Lord made heaven and earth, and RESTED on the seventh day, and was REFRESHED.**
> Exodus 31:16 TLB

In accordance with His divine nature, God cannot be exhausted in strength neither can He run out of fresh initiatives. Thus, there is no inevitability of retreat to restrategize or rest to reinforce. God only rested to show us a template on how to live here on earth. His rest does not reveal His nature. He needed to teach us how to walk in this world. The first line of Michael W. Smith's song, "Ancient word" perfectly captures this, "Holy words long preserved for our walk in this world".

The emphases in this book are so much in favour of hard work in order to achieve set goals. Nonetheless, you need to consciously rest and refresh in consonant with the template God has given us. Do all that is necessary to regain stature, vitality and wisdom. You need food to live. You need a shower and a good rest to be refreshed. You need to make time for relaxation so that you can last in the race. You need physical exercise to stay fit for the work. You need to throw a bit of fun to your activities to remain excited and happy.

You must have heard this proverb, "All work and no play makes Jack a dull boy." This proverb means a lot of things. If you do not consciously take time off from work for some reasonable measure of leisure, you will become both bored and boring. You can be worn out and become "a grief of mind" to other people (Gen. 26:35). So, do not take yourself to the dull stage; go for a break and refresh.

It is possible to work until all your strength is spent. This is actually where the law of diminishing return kicks in. Everyone starts work with a good level of capacity but with a continuous exertion of energy, it weakens to a breaking point thus bringing output to unacceptable margin. This is the mystery behind many sack letters. People work beyond their exhaustion points and start experiencing a rapid decline in their performances both in quality and in quantity. It will all be frustration if you want to drive your car when the fuel is spent. All you need is to refill your tank.

Do not bring yourself to a point of inertia. Always take time off from work and refresh yourself. Give attention to whatever helps you achieve this – food, rest, shower, medication, relaxation, a walk or any other form of work-aid pleasure. You will be a better man of higher performance and greater achievements if you learn God's lessons to rest and be refreshed. Many great achievers would have lived longer to do more exploit if they had adhered to this principle.

Look at what happened to the Maker of the earth when He put on flesh. "Jacob's well was there; and Jesus, tired from the long walk, sat wearily beside the well about noontime" (John 4:6 NLT). He rested here for rejuvenation and also sent for food. The Son of God can do without these but not the son of man.

> Therefore, at another point of fatigue,
> **And when they had sent away the multitude, they took him even as he was in the ship. And there were also with him other little ships. And there arose a great storm of wind, and the waves beat into the ship, so that it was now full. And he was in the hinder part of the ship, ASLEEP on a pillow...**
> Mark 4:36-38

After a lot of evangelistic work, Jesus' prescription for the apostles was rest.
> **And the apostles gathered themselves together unto Jesus, and told him all things, both what they had done, and what they had taught. And he said unto them, COME ye yourselves APART into a desert place, and REST a while: for there were many coming and going, and they had no leisure so much as to eat. And they departed into a desert place by ship privately.**
> Mark 6:30-32

At Gethsemane, they got to their breaking points. Every effort to pray was a struggle, in spite of Jesus Christ's plea for partnership and warning against temptation. Their spirits were very willing to pray, but their bodies were worn out. At the end, rest was still the answer.

> The Bible says,
> **Then cometh he to his disciples, and saith unto them, Sleep on now, and take your REST...**
> Matt. 26:45

One of the richest men in the world said that he switches off all his phones for 4 hours to deliberately rest in every 24 hours. Most achievers have similar arrangements. You also need your own rest plan. If people who have and control millions and billions of foreign and local currencies take time to rest and refresh themselves, you have no excuse whatsoever. There are no strict rules about this; just be wise enough to know when you need to take out time from work for leisure.

Rest is God's miracle for the rejuvenation of your soul and body. Sometimes I wonder at the level of reinforcement I get from a simple 5 to 10 minutes nap, a shower, and other refreshing rituals an hour before stepping out to speak in an event. It's something that always makes me feel brand-new. Do not drag your tired mind and body to a function where you are the focal person.

If you need my counsel then take one; work, work, work and rest and refresh. The God that made the Heaven and the earth keeps everlasting "pleasures" at His right hand (Ps. 16:11).

CHAPTER SIX

RESUME

Do not take time off from work and stay off permanently. That would be tantamount to REST IN PEACE. You recoup strength to resume work. You refresh to restart work. You reinforce to re-attack the enemies. You retreat to return to fight. You rejuvenate to continue the journey. You regain form to bounce back into the field. You recover your vitality to reclaim your position. You do not rest and run away.

Why does number eight stands for a new beginning? God rested on the seventh day and resumed work on the eighth day, and He has been working till now. No one knows the next time He would rest. All over the world and in all institutions, break time is brief and leave is for a definite period of time. You must consciously make every form of leisure to be brief and simple. You cannot achieve anything worthwhile if you major on pleasure at the expense of work.

You see, God worked for six days and rested for one day. One day in seven days is approximately 14 percent. It means, God wants work to take 86 percent of your time and other resources. Fourteen percent of 24 hours is still around the 4 hours we have been emphasizing. This is to let you understand that every form of pleasure and relaxation ought to be brief and little. It is not something that should take your entire day, night and resources. So, rest, be refreshed, and resume work.

Do not be satisfied prematurely; there must be something else to do. God resumed work after rest and planted a garden, established a fellowship and did many other things. The truth is, there is no end of accomplishment. There is no end to improving what you have already done. And so, there is no end to work; there is no end to making effort. This is why you need to retreat in order to regain strength and then resume work.

There are always more territories to be possessed when a man seems to have done his best.

> **Now Joshua was old and stricken in years; and the LORD said unto him, Thou art old and stricken in years, and there remaineth yet very much land to be possessed. This is the land that yet remaineth: all the borders of the Philistines, and all Geshuri,**
>
> **From Sihor, which is before Egypt, even unto the borders of Ekron northward, which is counted to the Canaanite: five lords of the Philistines; the Gazathites, and the Ashdothites, the Eshkalonites, the Gittites, and the Ekronites; also the Avites: From the south, all the land of the Canaanites, and Mearah that is beside the Sidonians, unto Aphek, to the borders of the Amorites:**
>
> **And the land of the Giblites, and all Lebanon, toward the sunrising, from Baal-gad under mount Hermon unto the entering into Hamath. All the inhabitants of the hill country from Lebanon unto Misrephoth-maim, and all the Sidonians...**
>
> Joshua 13:1-6

As long as you are alive, do not come to the end of your achievements. There is always more to achieve in life. Every additional day should translate to additional achievement. When everyone thinks you have done much, still do more. Do not stop working until you breathe your last breath. On his deathbed, John Wesley kept exhorting until he left. He repeatedly said to the people by his bedside, "The best of all is, God is with us." He said that until he gave up the ghost.

George Whitefield prayed, "Lord Jesus, I am weary in the work, but not of it. If I have yet finished my course, let me go and speak once in the field, seal the truth and come home and die." The Lord granted his request. His last sermon lasted two hours during which he cried out with the loudness of thunder before young people - "Work! Work!! A man to go to Heaven by works! I would as soon think of climbing to the moon on a robe of sand! How willing would I live forever to preach Christ, but I die to be with Him."

You cannot be through with work. More days mean more work. Paul the apostle who said he had finished his course yet kept writing letters that are relevant till date. The Lord Jesus Christ also said His work was finished on the cross but He kept reappearing to strengthen his men. The truth is, if a true achiever is still alive, he cannot stop working. An achiever can resign from his office but not from his work. Make up your mind to achieve something with your last breath. This is why you need to always return to work after every rest.

CHAPTER SEVEN

LOVING

I believe reading through this book has been an exciting journey for you. Before I draw the curtain, I would like to remind you of something very important in Pack 1, Item 2. God created the Heaven and the earth because He needed a place for His people. He had carried generations of people in His mind for too long. He intended manifesting them and habitations were needed. So, He created the Heaven and the earth as dwelling places for His people. Heaven is man's eternal home while earth is his temporary habitation.

You see, God was not stranded, lacking accommodation, before He created the Heaven and the earth. No. God lived, walked and worked before the both were created. He was not in need of accommodation. Earth is where man was sent to and Heaven is where man returns to. "Then shall the dust return to the earth as it was: and the spirit shall return unto God who gave it" (Eccl. 12:7). When man returns to God, he meets Him in Heaven.

Heaven is not where God is basking in the adulation of His creation and enjoying Himself. Heaven is God's waiting place. He waits for the daily return of His saints. Heaven is therefore a shared accommodation for God and His saints. The earth is a general gift to all the children of men. "The heaven, even the heavens, are the LORD's: but the earth hath he given to the children of men" (Ps. 115:16).

Look at this,
For thus saith the LORD that created the heavens; God himself that formed the earth and made it; he hath established it, he created it not in vain, he formed it to be inhabited: I am the LORD; and there is none else.
Isaiah 45:18

God's reason for making the Heaven and the earth was right because it was borne out of His loving disposition towards His people. You see, who you are determines what you do. Words, actions and reactions are perfect reflection of someone's nature. God is love and all He does demonstrate His love. A wicked man will do wickedly but "A good man sheweth favour..." (Ps. 112:5). God is love and He loves.

God does everything out of His love. Out of love for mankind, He made the Heaven and the earth. Out of love, He gave His only begotten Son. The Bible says, "For God so loved the world, that he gave his only begotten Son, that whosoever believeth in him should not perish, but have everlasting life" (John 3:16). Out of love, He is willing to do anything extra for the joy of humanity.

Look at Paul's question,
He that spared not his own Son, but delivered him up for us all, how shall he not with him also freely give us all things?
Rom. 8:32

When you consider the Heaven and the earth, God's loving disposition comes to the fore; it is so overwhelming. The vastness of the earth is only a glimpse of God's love for mankind. "May your roots go down deep into the soil of God's marvelous love. And may you have the power to understand, as all God's people should, how wide, how long, how high, and how deep his love really is. May you experience the love of Christ, though it is so great you will never fully understand it" (Eph. 3:18-19 NLT).

God does not do anything contrary to His love; His sole business is to demonstrate His love. He shows His love at all times and with every single act. "God demonstrates His own love toward us, in that while we were still sinners, Christ died for us" (Rom. 5:8 NKJV). It means, all of God's doings are acts of His love. The entire universe and all its elements are physical proofs of God's love for man.

Just as God is love, let the totality of your person be defined by love. And if you are love, you are as God in this world. Love is the real image of God. "God is love; and he that dwelleth in love dwelleth in God, and God in him. Herein is our love made perfect, that we may have boldness in the day of judgment: because as he is, so are we in this world" (1 John 4:16-17). If you are love, having a loving disposition towards people becomes a natural flow of your person.

Your nature confers on you the responsibility of expression. To put it simply, if you are love, you will always feel the need to do great things for humanity as an expression of your person. It is therefore a complete anomaly to build multiple estates with the mind to enslave people with rents. In consonant with my person, I ensure a signature of love in everything I do. This book is not written to extort money from the readers. Every word in this book carries a fragment of my love for the people of God on earth. No amount of money paid for it can make me feel fulfilled. The only thing that will give me fulfillment is that the readers rise to be God-like achievers.

Any person who diligently considers God's works and understands His favorable disposition towards man will surely be filled with awe. The Psalmist expressed his own surprise,

> **When I look at the sky, which you have made, at the moon and the stars, which you set in their places — what is man, that you think of him; mere man, that you care for him? Yet you made him inferior only to yourself; you crowned him with glory and honor. You appointed him ruler over everything you made; you placed him over all creation...**
>
> Ps 8:3-6 TEV

> Job also did,
>
> **What is man that you make so much of him, that you give him so much attention, that you examine him every morning and test him every moment?**
>
> Job 7:17-18 NIV

To be God's kind of achiever, you also need to be mindful of people. People should mean a great deal to you. People's lives should be precious in your eyes. King Saul said this when David spared his life for the second time. "I have sinned: return, my son David: for I will no more do thee harm, because my soul was precious in thine eyes this day: behold, I have played the fool, and have erred exceedingly" (1 Sam. 26:21).

God's kind of achiever should have the well-being of people as a priority. Your passion to achieve great feats ought to be people oriented. You ought to stop at nothing until you meet people's needs, solve their problems, answer their questions and settle their cases. The truth is, any achievement that does not put smiles on people's faces is only a mischief in God's sight. You will not live long to enjoy any achievement that is your setup to oppress the people of God.

Rehoboam lost his leadership of the entire Israel because he chose a mischievous path. He promised his people hell and the people took to their heels. He said, "My father made your yoke heavy, but I will add thereto: my father chastised you with whips, but I will chastise you with scorpions" (2 Chron. 10:14). God's kind of achievements do not make people to mourn; they rather make people to rejoice.

> The Israelites refused to be chastised with scorpions.
> **And when all Israel saw that the king would not hearken unto them, the people answered the king, saying, What portion have we in David? and we have none inheritance in the son of Jesse: every man to your tents, O Israel: and now, David, see to thine own house. So all Israel went to their tents.**
> 2 Chron. 10:16

Divinity and humanity will not be on your side if your achievements are platforms of wickedness to God's people. Just consider the fullness of the earth; God made all things for man's enjoyment. Out of His great love, He "giveth us richly ALL THINGS to enjoy" (1 Tim. 6:17). In all your accomplishments, your disposition should be to demonstrate your love to people and to make them full of joy.

> The Lord Jesus Christ constantly said,
> **These things have I spoken unto you, that my joy might remain in you, and that your JOY might be FULL.**
> **Hitherto have ye asked nothing in my name: ask, and ye shall receive, that your JOY may be FULL.**
> John 15:11, 16:24

At all times, God is interested in the fullness of the joy of His people. So, when He speaks and acts, He does so to express His love and to ensure the joy of the children of men. It is not far-fetched to say that God, out of His love, made the Heaven and the earth for the joy, comfort and pleasure of His people. You remember that, "enter thou into the JOY of thy lord" is Heaven's official welcome (Matt. 25:23). Let your own love create the joy of other people.

Paul the apostle exhorts us to "Do everything in love" (1 Cor. 16:14 NIV). This is "a more excellent way" to live (1 Cor. 12:31). This is how God lives. God does everything in love and you too should. Let all your achievements announce your love and not your greed. So, be love-driven with every effort you make to achieve great feats. This is the best way to follow God.

CHAPTER EIGHT

GIVING

Robert Louis Stevenson, a 19th century Scottish author, said, "You can give without loving but you never love without giving." The same quote was also attributed to Victor Hugo who lived within the same century. Victor Hugo added, "The great acts of love are done by those who are habitually performing small acts of kindness." If you have a loving disposition towards people, you will surely have a giving disposition. Generosity is the firstborn of love.

The very first offspring of God's love is giving. The Almighty is the most generous person in existence. The Bible says, "The earth hath he GIVEN to the children of men" (Ps. 115:16). The earth is God's love gift to mankind. Consider the sheer size of the earth and see God's nature towards giving to humanity. He gave a gift that countless generations over six millennia could not fully occupy. He gave a gift that the nearly seven billion people that currently live in it cannot exhaust its endowments. What an indescribable Giver!

The same disposition made His only begotten Son a gift to human race. The Bible says, "For God so loved the world, that he

GAVE his only begotten Son..." (John 3:16). The same God is still willing to give anything to man if it furthers His happiness. "He that SPARED NOT his own Son, but DELIVERED him up for us all, how shall he not with him also freely GIVE us all things?" (Rom. 8:32). He "GIVETH us richly all things to enjoy" (1 Tim. 6:17).

A diligent consideration of God's works is an exploration of His giving character. So great is His love and so massive is His giving. The Almighty is a giving God and you need to be a giving man to be His kind of achiever. You need to be disposed to giving bountifully to other people. I was studying the life and calling of Abraham some time ago and I wondered at His generosity. Why should a man kill a fat calf for only three men?

> Look at it,
> **And Abraham ran unto the herd, and fetcht a calf tender and good, and gave it unto a young man; and he hasted to dress it. And he took butter, and milk, and the calf which he had dressed, and set it before them; and he stood by them under the tree, and they did eat.**
> Gen. 18:7-8

It is not a surprise that God called Abraham His friend. If you are well acquainted with the Scriptures you will understand that all that Abraham achieved typified God's kind of achievements. Most great achievers are bountiful givers to their people and you should not be different.

No one will be financially fat enough to achieve great feats without possessing the virtue of liberality. Stinginess drains a man like dry gin. No tight-fisted person ever achieves or sustains something worthwhile. The laws that govern the entire universe do not work in favour of parsimonious people.

The Bible says,
There is that scattereth, and yet increaseth; and there is that withholdeth more than is meet, but it tendeth to poverty. The liberal soul shall be made fat: and he that watereth shall be watered also himself.
Prov. 11:24-25

What you give is invariably proportionate to who you are; and the extent of your prosperity is proportionate to what you give. You cannot give to your people like an ant and hope to become an elephant in their midst. That is the very antithesis of scriptural principles on financial prosperity. It is written, "He which soweth sparingly shall reap also sparingly; and he which soweth bountifully shall reap also bountifully" (2 Cor. 9:6). I believe you know that it is bountiful reaping that empowers achievers for incredible accomplishments.

The truth is, you have no future if you are not a habitual giver to your people. What you enjoy after many years is not merely what you save but what you give. Great achievers are made by the massive return of what they gave. The Bible says, "Cast thy bread upon the waters: for thou shalt find it after many days. Give a portion to seven, and also to eight; for thou knowest not what evil shall be upon the earth. In the morning sow thy seed, and in the evening withhold not thine hand..." (Eccl. 11:1-6).

You cannot achieve anything of significance if your bosom is empty. Truly, it is your giving that guarantees the fullness of your bosom. The Maker of the Heaven and the earth said, "Give, and it shall be given unto you; good measure, pressed down, and shaken together, and running over, shall men give into your bosom. For with the same measure that ye mete withal it shall be measured to you again" (Luke 6:38). God has the divine mechanism to make people give into the giver's bosom.

Cheerful givers please God and He influences people in their favour.

> **God loveth a cheerful giver. When a man's ways please the LORD, he maketh even his enemies to be at peace with him. The king's heart is in the hand of the LORD, as the rivers of water: he turneth it whithersoever he will.**
> 2 Cor. 9:7, Prov. 16:7, 21:1

If you have made up your mind to be God's kind of achiever, go ahead and give generously to your people. God constructed the earth and donated it to humanity. You can build a city, a village, an estate or something massive and donate it to your people. If these are too much for you, you can dig boreholes, build community halls, grade village pathways, and build community clinics or classrooms. If these are still too much for you, you can put something else together for your people.

Where would you have been if God had not provided the earth? You are enjoying what God gave; it therefore behoves you to ensure that other people enjoy your munificence. If you want to be God's kind of achiever, you need to provide yourself as a channel of His blessings. No reservoir of God's blessings remains good enough for further divine supply. The giving nature positions you in the light of God's favour. This is why the saying is true that GIVERS NEVER LACK.

CHAPTER NINE

BLESSING

Giving goes beyond handing out physical things to passing on invisible things. As a matter of fact, people give more than they really know they do because most of the things they give are intangible. Giving things that are invisible is a more powerful way of making impact in people's lives. Words are some of the invisible materials we give to people on a daily basis. It is unfortunate that most people dispense more evil words than good.

Blessing is a group of words released to empower people while a curse is also a group of words released to impoverish people. From the church to the world at large, individuals impoverish people with words than they empower them.

Every day, words are performed in people's lives, whether they are good or evil. Words exist as spirits when spoken into the unseen realm. The Lord Jesus said, "The words that I speak unto you, they are spirit..." (John 6:63). Spoken words must fulfill their mission if they are not disabled by higher words.

Actually, all manner of material things we give are gifts. Blessing is a group of words that communicate life and strength. Abraham gave words of blessing to Isaac while he gave material things (gifts) to his other sons. He blessed Isaac and assisted the others. "Abraham gave all that he had unto Isaac" by laying his hands on him and speaking words into his life (Gen. 25:5).

> Look at what the Bible says further,
> **But unto the sons of the concubines, which Abraham had, Abraham gave GIFTS, and sent them away from Isaac his son, while he yet lived, eastward, unto the east country.**
>
> Gen. 25:6

It will interest you to know that all that Jacob and Esau were struggling for were words, not physical wealth. Look at what two individuals battled for from their mother's wombs to adulthood, "God give thee of the dew of heaven, and the fatness of the earth, and plenty of corn and wine: Let people serve thee, and nations bow down to thee: be lord over thy brethren, and let thy mother's sons bow down to thee: cursed be every one that curseth thee, and blessed be he that blesseth thee" (Gen. 27:28-29).

There is a gross misplacement of value and priority in our time. People value wealth more than words of blessing. People struggle for their parents' property and despise their last words of blessing. What they fail to realize is that words can produce wealth but wealth cannot produce words.

The visible cannot produce the invisible. It is completely the other way round; the unseen give birth to the seen. The Bible says, the "things which are seen were not made of things which do appear" (Heb. 11:3). Those who seek blessing seek words of power and not tangible materials.

God gave man gifts and blessing. The earth is God's gift "to the children of men" (Ps. 115:16). The blessing of the LORD is His life and His power released by words to man in order to fully maximize the earth. "There the LORD commanded the blessing, even life for evermore. Where the word of a king is, there is power…" (Eccl. 8:4, Ps. 133:3). "The blessing of the LORD, it maketh rich, and he addeth no sorrow with it" (Prov. 10:22).

Consciously, "God blessed them, and God said unto them, Be fruitful, and multiply, and replenish the earth, and subdue it: and have dominion over the fish of the sea, and over the fowl of the air, and over every living thing that moveth upon the earth" (Gen 1:28). God has a high disposition towards empowering His people. "Thou shalt remember the LORD thy God: for it is he that giveth thee power to get wealth" (Deut. 8:18).

There are three things I would like you to note here. Firstly, God blessed them and SAID unto them. There cannot be the blessing without the saying. "And God blessed Noah and his sons, and SAID unto them…" (Gen. 9:1). It is the saying that makes the life and the power available.

Secondly, the blessing is not a tangible thing. All things that can be seen and touched are gifts that come "from the Father of lights, with whom is no variableness, neither shadow of turning" (James 1:17).

Thirdly, the blessing gives birth to gifts but it cannot be the other way round. The power is the blessing; wealth and riches are gifts. Look at this, "Through faith also Sara herself received STRENGTH to conceive seed, and was delivered of a child when she was past age, because she judged him faithful who had promised" (Heb. 11:11). The strength is the blessing; the baby is a gift. The Bible says, "Children are a gift from God..." (Ps. 127:3 TLB).

What you have learnt points to the fact that there is so much to what you say. The Bible says, "Death and life are in the power of the tongue: and they that love it shall eat the fruit thereof" (Prov. 18:21). Set your heart to bless people and you will always do. You cannot be favourably disposed to blessing people and end up cursing them. No. It is what saturates your heart that flow from your mouth. "Out of the abundance of the heart the mouth speaketh" (Matt. 12:34).

I believe so many people would have risen to greatness if you had learned to consistently speak words of life to them. I believe, "I have received commandment to bless" people and I do it with everything in me (Num. 23:20). The Bible says, "A city becomes great when righteous men give it their blessing..." (Prov. 11:11 TEV). You can join the holy business of giving people the blessing. It is about speaking to people words that God confirms and establishes.

> Look at this,
> **And they** (Rebecca's brother, mother and relatives) **blessed Rebekah, and said unto her, Thou art our sister, be thou the mother of thousands of millions, and let thy seed possess the gate of those which hate them.**
> Gen. 24:60

I like these words, David "blessed the people in the name of the LORD of hosts... David returned to bless his household..." (2 Sam. 6:18, 20). This is the way of God's kind of achievers – empowering people by speaking life to them. You need to also be a man that blesses people in and out of your house. If you do not know any other thing to say, continue to say, "The LORD bless thee, and keep thee: The LORD make his face shine upon thee, and be gracious unto thee: The LORD lift up his countenance upon thee, and give thee peace" (Num. 6:24-26).

Do not forget that the man God empowered is the one developing the earth over the six millennia. I have also learned by experience that the people you bless will turn round to be a blessing to you. So, bless people no matter what they do for you or to you. Paul the apostle exhorted, "Bless them which persecute you: bless, and curse not" (Rom. 12:14). Cursing people is creating more problems in the world; so bless, bless and bless.

Bless people, especially your own people. I bless my family members; I speak over them words that God always command to come to pass (Lam. 3:37). I bless the people God sends to be with me in our church. No matter how short the service, I bless the people in the name of the LORD and there is great performance. The Lord Jesus Christ continued to bless "his own" until His last minute on earth (John 13:1).

> The Bible says,
> **And he led them out as far as to Bethany, and he lifted up his hands, and BLESSED THEM. And it came to pass, while HE BLESSED THEM, he was parted from them, and carried up into heaven.**
> Luke 24:50-51

Do not impoverish your own, but rather empower them by giving them your blessing. The LORD said, "By my blessing they will increase in numbers; my blessing will bring them honor" (Jer. 30:19 TEV).

Do not wait for your last breath; start blessing your people now. Always say to them, you shall not die, but live, and declare the works of the LORD. You shall flourish like the palm tree. My God shall supply all your need according to His riches in glory by Christ Jesus. The grace of our Lord Jesus Christ be with you. Amen.

CHAPTER TEN

CROWNING

ook at this, "When I look at the sky, which you have made, at the moon and the stars, which you set in their places - what is man, that you think of him; mere man, that you care for him? Yet you made him inferior only to yourself; you CROWNED him with glory and honor. You appointed him ruler over everything you made; you placed him over all creation" (Ps. 8:3-6 TEV).

> Look at the same verse from the King James Version,
> **Thou...hast CROWNED him with glory and honour. Thou madest him to have dominion over the works of thy hands; thou hast put all things under his feet...**
> Ps. 8:5-6

Another disposition the Maker of the Heaven and the earth shows towards people is that of crowning them. He blessed man and crowned him with glory and honour. The Almighty does not seek ways to disgrace His own and you should not do that either. There are people who take so much pleasure in disgracing other people. They are excited when they embarrass others. This way of life is absolutely antithetical to that of great achievers.

God is in the business of crowning; that is, glorifying and honouring people. He is in the business of uniting His honour with His people. He said, "I will multiply them and they will not be diminished; I will also honor them and they will not be insignificant" (Jer. 30:19 NASU). He told Moses in favour of Joshua in Numbers 27:20, "Thou shalt put some of thine honour upon him".

Consider the same verse,
Transfer your authority to him so the whole community of Israel will obey him. Publicly give him your authority so that all the people of Israel will obey him.
Num. 27:20 NLT & TLB

If you want to be an achiever of lasting relevance, you need to be a man committed to honouring people. Honouring a man is as putting a royal crown on His head. What a good feeling! Do you remember the prescription of Haman about who the king delighted to honour? It was a prescription to catch a royal feeling.

Look at this,
So Haman came in. And the king said unto him, What shall be done unto the man whom the king delighteth to honour? Now Haman thought in his heart, To whom would the king delight to do honour more than to myself? And Haman answered the king, For the man whom the king delighteth to honour, Let the royal apparel be brought which the king useth to wear, and the horse that the king rideth upon, and the crown royal which is set upon his head:

And let this apparel and horse be delivered to the hand of one of the king's most noble princes, that they may

array the man withal whom the king delighteth to honour, and bring him on horseback through the street of the city, and proclaim before him, Thus shall it be done to the man whom the king delighteth to honour. Then the king said to Haman, Make haste, and take the apparel and the horse, as thou hast said, and do even so to Mordecai the Jew, that sitteth at the king's gate: let nothing fail of all that thou has spoken.
Esther 6:6-10

Crowning is the business of honouring people and giving them the feeling of importance. It was Maya Angelou who said, "I have learned that people will forget what you said, people will forget what you did, but people will never forget how you made them feel." God does and enjoys the business of making His people feel good, and most achievers do the same thing. It is only mean fellows that always make others feel like they are nothing but pesky insects and stinking vermin. You can make people feel the royalty of God in them by crowing them with glory and honour.

There are many ways to make people feel good. God used the way of leadership; He put Adam and Eve in charge of all things; He made them masters of all things; He made them lords over all the works of His hands. God told them with finality, "You are masters; I am putting you in charge; have dominion; rule over" all the works of my hands (Gen. 1:28). If you were the direct recipients of this authorization, how would you feel?

What do you see in the words of the Almighty? Great repose of confidence in the people He made; great appreciation for their global capacity; and great honour for their persons. This is not what any man can buy; God does it out of His pleasure. He enjoys honouring people. Paul the apostle said, "No man taketh this honour unto himself, but he that is called of God…" (Heb. 5:4). Adam and Eve did not apply for this, no; God did it in accord with His nature.

There are things that are natural with God. The Psalmist said, "Look upon me and be merciful to me, as your custom is (as is your way, as you always do, after your manner, as it is your tradition) toward those who love your name" (Ps. 119:132). Just like showing mercy to His lovers, crowning people with glory and honour is God's custom. You need to also have such tradition of honouring people. Do not allow anyone leave your presence feeling ill about his person.

You need to understand that the disposition of others affects your speed of achievement. The truth is, your disposition births the disposition of others. If you make others feel they are rats, they will behave like rats towards you. If you do not want that then treat people with honour as they ought to be treated. If you make people feel they are princes and princesses, you will surely get a harvest of a kingly disposition from them.

God made man god and keeps reaping a harvest of referential worship from him. He made man master and thus secured his loyalty and service. You cannot be busy humiliating people and have them work for your own lifting. If you want to fall woefully, make all the people around you feel awful. If you want to rise, inspire the people around you. Truthfully speak of their virtues in the way they will feel honoured; put them in charge of position of honour; appreciate their presence, efforts and appearance.

If a man thinks he is "fearfully and wonderfully made", do not say or do anything that will make Him feel otherwise. Do not be the axe against people's self-esteem; you will be the enemy of all. When it comes to honour, forget about yourself and pour it all on others and be rest assured that you will like the harvest. It was Paul the apostle who exhorts us to "be kindly affectioned one to another with brotherly love; in honour preferring one another" (Rom. 12:10).

Join this business of crowning people and you will be the man of the people and of great achievements. You may not need to do much; a compliment will be okay for each individual you meet daily. It was Abraham Lincoln who said, "Everybody likes a compliment." If everybody likes a compliment, everybody will definitely like its giver. Wherever you are, do not be the accuser of the brethren lest you will be treated like the devil.

Mother Teresa said, "The biggest disease today is not leprosy and tuberculosis but rather the feeling of being unwanted." Let every man and woman you meet be your own Adam and Eve and be sure you crown them with glory and honour as God did. As a matter of priority, do all you can righteously to make them feel they are greatly loved and highly appreciated. I believe you will achieve far more than you dream.

CHAPTER ELEVEN

FEEDING

Another great disposition of God towards mankind is that of making comprehensive arrangement for nourishment. The Almighty knew from the very beginning that man will "live by bread" (Deut. 8:3). I believe God did not want man to suffer for food any day. He therefore made provision for food before He formed man. Man became a living soul and found enough food waiting for him. What a caring Father!

> And God said,
> **Look! I have given you the seed-bearing plants throughout the earth and all the fruit trees for your food.**
> Gen 1:29 NLT

When the Maker of all things was here on earth, He fed people in their thousands. He was always instructing His disciples to "give ye them to eat" (Mark 6:37). "Jesus said unto them, They need not depart; give ye them to eat" (Matt. 14:16). The people of the earth came to Him and He nourished them spiritually, morally and physically. There had never been a time or generation that

God failed to include a welfare arrangement in His programme for man.

The Almighty took His people on a forty year journey and He fed them all through.

He had commanded the clouds from above, and opened the doors of heaven, And had rained down manna upon them to eat, and had given them of the corn of heaven. Man did eat angels' food: he sent them meat to the full.

He caused an east wind to blow in the heaven: and by his power he brought in the south wind. He rained flesh also upon them as dust, and feathered fowls like as the sand of the sea: And he let it fall in the midst of their camp, round about their habitations.
Ps. 78:23-28

You must understand that the greater the achievement you seek, the more people you need. There is nothing great you can achieve all alone. You do not achieve more to need fewer people. Greater achievement is about getting more people. The truth is, you become more and more dependent on people with every step forward. This is why you need to consciously develop a caring disposition towards people.

You need to be a man that is always mindful of the well-being of the people God sends your way. You should have the purest concern for what they eat, where they live and what they wear. Can you feel what the greatest Achiever said in Matthew 15:32, "I have compassion on the multitude, because they continue with me now three days, and have nothing to eat: and I will not send them away fasting, lest they faint in the way."

Every true achiever I have ever known is exactly like the Lord in this regard. They are always moved with compassion when they see people suffering for the most basic needs of life. This is the reason why they are natural philanthropists. They feed thousands of people through remuneration and charity. Being favourably disposed to human well-being is crucial if you want to be one of the greatest achievers of your time.

People are more committed to you when they know you care about their welfare. Other people died and the Jews buried them straight away. Why did they keep the corpse of Dorcas and seek for someone to bring her back to life? It was an expression of their commitment to her because of her care for them. I believe you know what happened when Peter the apostle got to where the corpse was? "All the widows stood by him weeping, and shewing the coats and garments which Dorcas made, while she was with them" (Acts 9:39).

It was John Cassis who said, "Nobody cares how much you know until they know how much you care." You will surely have more committed people around you if you are highly disposed to caring for people's needs. Ralph W. Emerson said, "All mankind love a lover." You can afford to be a lover of humanity; the good thing about this is that humanity will love you back. The love of mankind will always translate to greater achievement.

God gives greater blessing to the man that has many mouths to feed. The provision of an object of blessing is not the same with that of a channel of blessing. An object of blessing collect provision for his sole mouth but the channel of blessing collects for himself and the multitude with him. God blesses the object but blesses people through the channel. The object receives single blessing, the channel receives block blessing.

I believe most lasting entrepreneurial achievers are collecting divine provision on behalf of thousand and millions of people they pay and help. As a potential achiever, you need to ask yourself: Do I really care about people? At present, how many people do I have on my payroll? How many people are on my charity list? It is vain to expect too much from God when you do not have many people to cater for.

Disposition is a thing of the mind. You may not have anyone on your payroll right now but you can prepare your mind to care for people. If your mind is set on caring for people, you will care for many people before you know it. Actually, it does not take so much to care for people. You can start with the little you have and be rest assured that "God is able to give you more than you need, so that you will always have all you need for yourselves and more than enough for every good cause" (2 Cor. 9:8 TEV).

CHAPTER TWELVE

THANKING

See, "God looked over all that he had made, and it was excellent in every way. This ended the sixth day" (Gen. 1:31 TLB). Everyone and everything cooperated with God to have the most gigantic project ever undertaken and completed on schedule. I thought to myself, what else did the Lord do on the sixth day after supervising and confirming that His works were perfect? I believe He went round giving all a pat at the back.

> The Maker of the earth taught,
> **After a long time the lord of those servants cometh, and reckoneth with them. And so he that had received five talents came and brought other five talents, saying, Lord, thou deliveredst unto me five talents: behold, I have gained beside them five talents more. His lord said unto him, WELL DONE, thou good and faithful servant: thou hast been faithful over a few things, I will make thee ruler over many things: enter thou into the joy of thy lord.**
>
> Matt. 25:19-21

The "lord" in this parable refers to God. God appreciates people who perform well in His cause. God is the Institutor of the reward system. "He is a rewarder of them that diligently seek him" (Heb. 11:6). God has a well done, a thank you and a crown waiting for each labourer. As you learnt earlier, Heaven is not God's hiding place; it is rather a thank you venue for the people that remain true to him to the end.

> Paul the apostle said,
> **I have fought long and hard for my Lord, and through it all I have kept true to him. And now the time has come for me to stop fighting and rest. In heaven a crown is waiting for me, which the Lord, the righteous Judge, will give me on that great day of his return.**
> 2 Tim. 4:7 TLB

The truth is, God will not tell us to live how He does not live nor instruct us to do what He does not do himself. He tells us to be holy because He is holy. "Ye shall be holy: for I the LORD your God am holy" (Lev. 19:2). He tells us to be merciful because He is merciful. "The LORD is merciful and gracious, slow to anger, and plenteous in mercy" (Ps. 103:8). He tells us to "be thankful" because He is thankful (Ps. 100:4).

The Almighty gives kudos to the efforts of His people. He has a package of appreciation for each labourer (Matt. 20:1-16). He appreciates the contribution of His workforce and He rewards their diligence. If you want to be a lasting achiever, thankfulness must be a core virtue. J. H. Jowett said, "Every virtue divorced from thankfulness is maimed." It means thankfulness is the health of all the virtues of achievement.

It was Max De Pree who said, "The first responsibility of a leader is to define reality. The last is to say thank you." Unlike God, none of us can take absolute credit for our achievement. We achieve great feat by the life and the help we are given. God gave us life and men gave us help. We owe God and people thanks for being a part of our strides. Even people we hire deserve kudos for diligently doing the jobs they were paid to do.

You need to understand that no good input is unworthy of thanks. Do not show an iota of ingratitude and unkindness to anyone that has contributed to your success. In different ways, express your gratitude to God and people that have stood with you through thick and thin. To despise people that have played a role in your life and destiny is tantamount to standing in your own way or shooting yourself in the foot. You cannot go forward. In order to enjoy a continuous advancement in life, you must maintain an attitude of gratitude towards your partners or people that have helped you previously.

At all times, be grateful for every contribution people make in your life. Thankfulness is an expression of gratitude. You can only express gratitude if you have it. For this reason, George Herbert prayer should be your daily desire. "Thou O Lord hast given so much to me, give me one more thing – a grateful heart." The answer to this prayer should translate to a lifestyle of deliberately placing value on people and their inputs to your cause.

If you are grateful and you can express it to God and the people He uses to advance you, then get ready for greater things. It was James Allen who said, "No duty is more urgent than that of returning thanks." If you can return thanks, you can retain helpers.

Look at this,

And Jesus answering said, Were there not ten cleansed? but where are the nine? There are not found that returned to give glory to God, save this stranger. And he said unto him, Arise, go thy way: thy faith hath made thee whole.

Luke 17:17-19

If you retain helpers, you will have more help. If you have more help, you will achieve more. So, always end every project with a thank you arrangement and there will be no end to your achievements.

ACTION

A 19th century English philosopher, Herbert Spencer said, "The great aim of education is not knowledge but action." All you have learnt in this book will mean nothing if they are just for storage in your mind. In a short time from now, the knowledge you have acquired can translate to landmark achievements if you act on them. I urge you to reread this book, this time, not for knowledge but for action. See how you can act on these 60 items. I believe you will achieve things like God.

The wisdom of God in Genesis chapter one is inexhaustible. What you have learnt in this book may be less than one percent of the mysteries of creation. It will be better to go beyond this book to the God of creation. It will be enough if this book stimulates you to seek God's ways of achievement. I believe there are more revelation about God's achieving traits you need to catch. So, ask the Holy Spirit to teach you more and achieve more than you ever dream.

I hope to see you in GOGA; it is the Gathering Of Great Achievers.